Naughty Step Alternatives: An Illustrated Guide for Parents who want to Improve Bothersome Behaviour

By Mandy Stopard and Kent Tayler

Published by Lyvit Publishing, Cornwall

www.lyvit.com

ISBN 978-0-9957979-7-0

For Brenda and Maurice
I've missed talking to you about the book.
Wish you were here.

(from Mandy)

For Stacey, with love forever.

(from Kent)

Naughty Step Alternatives:
An Illustrated Guide for Parents
who want to Improve Bothersome
Behaviour

Contents

Introduction: key principles, and how to make use of this book

Lots of parents struggle with the behaviour of their children, and always have done. Thankfully, the days of overbearing and dictatorial parenting are behind us, but children do not always behave in the way we want them to, or in a way which leaves them happy and settled.

Kids don't come with a manual:

...and now we tend to talk more openly about our concerns and look harder for answers...

But it's easy to get overwhelmed and confused by the range of information and advice that is out there.

So this book aims to be a straightforward, practical guide to managing and improving children's behaviour. It looks at the situations where bothersome behaviour commonly occurs and provides practical tips – either to prevent it happening, or ways of dealing with it when it does happen.

All of the advice and suggestions have been tried and tested by parents, and in our experience they improve children's behaviour when applied with perseverance and consistency.

Beyond the 'naughty step'

The 'naughty step' phrase is commonly used now, and when we work with parents it is the behaviour improvement technique they nearly always talk about. While it works for some families, the atmosphere can become negative if children don't respond immediately, or if it's the only strategy that parents use. Children sometimes end up gaining a lot of attention for difficult behaviour as parents repeatedly place their agitated offspring back on the designated spot. Such negative attention can make matters worse, 'reinforcing' unwanted behaviour as a child finds that during the naughty-step implementation saga they are the centre of the household…and not in a good way! This can quickly lead to everyone getting angry and frustrated.

The 'naughty step' (or the less stigmatising 'time-out' term) may have a valid place as part of a positive plan and can be effective if children and their parents have skills in calming themselves. But it isn't the only answer and never has been. That's why this book offers a range of alternatives, with an emphasis on preventing negative behaviours happening in the first place, and also tips for a wider repertoire of responses to those difficult moments which every parent experiences.

Key Principles

The fundamental principle behind all the guidance in this book is that the solutions to children's behaviour lie with parents and how they behave. Parents who are determined to alter the way they communicate and respond to their children usually have more success than parents who see all the problem as residing in the child, or people who just keep their fingers crossed and hope their kids will 'grow out of it'.

A number of other principles and building blocks for improving behaviour flow from this:

Be a role model

If we want our children to be caring and calm people it is helpful to show them, as best we can, how to be rational, composed, understanding and empathic.

Become a behaviour 'coach'

Seeing unwanted behaviour as a sign that a child lacks emotional, social and behavioural skills and recognising that these skills can be taught is a great step in making progress with behaviour.

Anticipate issues and take pre-emptive action to prevent problems

Prevention is better than cure! Correcting unwanted behaviour will often bring attention to it which can then reinforce and strengthen it, making the behaviour more likely to reoccur. A calm, trouble-free environment supports positive behaviour so it is helpful, where possible, to take measures which avoid the issues starting in the first place.

Stay positive and provide lots of good attention

Children who get lots of negative 'telling off' attention often repeat irritating behaviours. Giving more attention when things are going well (as opposed to when there are difficulties and challenges) and avoiding branding children as 'bad' in some way will improve their behaviour.

Create structure and routines, and communicate clear expectations

Many children misbehave because it isn't clear what they need to do, especially if boundaries change from day to day, or even moment to moment. Clarity about expectations and establishing sensible routines keeps everyone feeling more secure and less tempted to try to control situations.

Take prompt and 'proportionate' action

Responding to unwanted behaviour in a 'measured', mild-mannered but firm way supports children in understanding what is expected, and reduces the confusion and resentment associated with the 'mixed message approach'. The muddle of consequences borne out of frustration, empty threats or simply avoiding addressing the problems can usefully be replaced with a more consistent, considered approach.

How to make use of this book

'Naughty Step Alternatives' is a visual, light read designed to support parents who are looking for straightforward, accessible, authoritative guidance and may not have the time or energy for reading a lengthy tome on the subject.

Each chapter is devoted to showing how the principles can be applied to discrete issues commonly reported by parents of children in the pre-school year and during the primary school phase. The principles can be adapted for older children, but the illustrations and examples focus on children aged 4-9 years. The final chapter provides a summary of some key things to remember to do - and also things to avoid.

Within each chapter there are two main sections. The first is 'prevention' - we see these measures as paramount as it's always preferable to 'head off' bothersome behaviour before it becomes a problem, and so avoid the stress of crisis management. So readers might want to check out these prevention strategies before becoming too focused on the second section in each chapter, which describes ways of dealing with the difficulties when they have occurred.

The guidance takes the form of tips and suggestions, with many of the strategies conveyed through illustrations of families. This is a device for communicating the ideas, and all the illustrations portray imaginary characters. But the situations depicted, and the guidance for dealing with them, are based on real life experience of working with parents and building up a picture of what is effective.

The book can be used in a 'dipping in and out' way, looking at chapters which correspond with the issues of the moment. Or you can read it cover to cover to get a broader oversight. You will notice some common threads running through the tips and guidance on all the different issues. It generally helps to make a plan - either for preventing bothersome behaviour, or for responding to it when it happens - and to talk to your child about it and get them involved. You can make some adaptations along the way, but things work well when there is a clear focus on the behaviour you want to see, and the plan is followed through. When dealing with difficulties, the main things to remember are to deal calmly and decisively with challenges, and to carry out some post-incident teaching or 'debrief'. You will know what is relevant to your situation and your child!

Meet your authors, Mandy and Kent

All About Mandy:

Mandy has been a teacher for longer than she cares to remember! Her work at 'the chalk face' as a classroom teacher lasted for over 20 demanding but wonderful years. She has held managerial roles in schools; jobs which majored on supporting children to improve their behaviour and social and emotional skills. As a local authority 'Behaviour Advisory Teacher' she gained more expertise in the 'behaviour field' with a range of schools and families and is now enjoying her freelance work as a consultant to schools and parents. Helping parents to 'calm things down' in their own homes is proving to be a great way to deploy all the advantageous behaviour strategies gathered over a long career. More about her work can be found at www.behaviourspecialist.co.uk.

Some Testimonials - fictitious characters, factual endorsements

MANDY'S INPUT HAS COMPLETELY CHANGED OUR FAMILY LIFE FOR THE BETTER!

HER ADVICE, TIPS AND STRATEGIES HAVE BEEN INVALUABLE. I'VE BECOME A BETTER PARENT AND HAVE A HAPPIER CHILD. SHE'S JUST BRILLIANT!

THANK YOU MANDY FOR GETTING OUR FAMILY BACK ON TRACK AND FOR FINDING THE PRACTICAL SOLUTIONS WE NEEDED TO MOVE FORWARD.

FROM YOUR DOWN TO EARTH AND CLEAR ADVICE, WE COULD TELL YOU HAD EXPERIENCE AS A TEACHER AND A MUM. WE WERE LUCKY TO MEET YOU!

This is Kent:

Kent is a professional cartoonist whose career started many moons ago drawing gag cartoons for The Sun. Since then, he's best known for his work in Viz comic, Private Eye, Prospect and The New European (amongst many others). And being a father himself, he fully understands the challenges of parenthood (and has the grey hairs to prove it!)

So what follows is a collection of top tips to successfully support children to stay calm, be cooperative and move towards being pleasant and contented human beings.

Chapter 1: Attention Please!

Children's need for attention underlies much of the bothersome behaviour that parents talk to us about. Attention-seeking, in a negative manner, is a result of a child's perception that they aren't getting noticed. Any attention, even being 'told off', nagged or shouted at, helps to meet their need to be important and remarkable in their parents' eyes.

Parents often feel they give their children lots of attention, but it's worth checking what kind of communication goes on most in the family. A downward spiral may form in families where children experience more and more negativity from their parents for poor and uncooperative behaviour; this then leads to the children, in need of being noticed, creating more situations which result in attention, even if it is negative or unpleasant. Positivity gets squeezed out, and the whole thing starts again. Breaking this cycle is key to improving behaviour and calming things down.

MY CHILD MAKES A FUSS AND IS DIFFICULT AND UNCOOPERATIVE WHEN I AM BUSY OR MY ATTENTION IS ELSEWHERE

It may look like this:

Prevention

Giving good quality attention

Pro-actively provide frequent positive attention when things are going 'okay'

Parents find this simple step really effective in preventing difficult behaviour. Connecting with children before they start to misbehave or come seeking attention, helps to keep things calm. Getting in there early and just being in their company in a calm and pleasant way, either playing, sharing an activity, chatting, or merely sitting alongside them can work wonders. When things are calm, those parents who can take the lead from their children and fit in with what they are doing, rather than 'being in command' often have the most success in letting their kids know they don't need to 'play up' to get noticed.

HAVE I PAID ATTENTION TO MY CHILD LATELY?

Engage fully with the child after a break in contact

Sharing a few 'quality' moments when they first get up in the morning, or straight after school, can support more settled behaviour as a result of the child feeling valued and important.

Sometimes children don't seem keen to have attention or may avoid answering their parents' questions, especially after a busy day at school; this may be a result of tiredness or a need to focus on something else after an intense time.

In these cases, just being present can be helpful in meeting the underlying attention needs of a reluctant youngster. Merely watching them play and commenting occasionally to show you are focused on what they're doing will support an understanding that you are placing them high up on your agenda, and there's absolutely no need to seek out attention in a negative way to get noticed .

Praise them!

Watch out for small signs of appropriate behaviour in situations when difficult attention-seeking behaviour has happened previously and comment favourably, or 'catch them being good' (as the Americans say). Praise has the most impact when it specifically describes the behaviour rather than being too general, e.g. 'You settled to your homework on your own for 5 minutes; that's good concentration', rather than a mere: 'good work!'

This will feed and 'reinforce' the behaviour you are wanting to promote; parents find they get more of what they focus on.

Prepare for the end of the attention session

The double whammy of wanting more and more of a good thing (nice attention) and a dislike of transitions (any tricky change) may tip your previously settled child over the edge (see chapter 2 for more on managing transitions).

Some children soak up attention like a sponge and won't easily let go.

So from the very start of a shared activity it can help to be clear about how long you can stick around. During the activity be mindful of when you need to withdraw and as the attention time is coming to an end, provide advance warnings or countdowns. If necessary prepare your child with an activity to do in your absence and tell them when the attention will be re-instated.

Make a plan

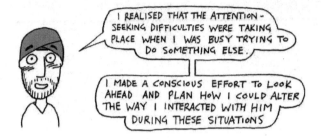

Many parents find that things improve if they identify when their child shows difficult attention-seeking behaviour and formulate some strategies for when the situation comes up again.

This plan will be more effective if it incorporates some of the following aspects:

'Paying-in' some good quality attention just prior to potentially tricky situations

For example, if the problem involves your child wanting attention after being settled in the evening, ensure the bedtime routine is 'warm and cuddly' and there are plenty of opportunities to 'connect'.

Reading a book and providing physical affection before 'lights out' will support your child in managing without attention after you have left.

'Paying-in' positive attention 'moments' during tricky situations

Planning in advance to show your child some good attention at regular and frequent intervals during the situations you have identified is often effective in heading off unwanted behaviour. Short bursts of positivity and gentle connection make for pleasant moments which prompt children to feel secure, and that they are still being appreciated even when they are expected to follow instructions or be a bit self-sufficient.

Children may either stall or behave badly during routines, chores or outings because the parent is busy doing their own thing and isn't fully keyed-in and meeting the child's need for positive attention. Regular and predictable reassuring moments can prevent irritating behaviour which may be an attempt to get the parent to take notice or a sign of anxiety because the child feels on their own.

Share the plan and give them a say

We find that parents who share the salient points of their plan with their child prior to the situation are more effective in gaining progress with behaviour. Picking a calm moment to explain clearly about what will happen next (the structure and sequence of the situation coming up), and the behaviour which is needed, helps to establish boundaries which may have previously been a bit vague or missing altogether. This preparation, when the atmosphere is conducive, supports the child to accept expectations and feel more secure about what is going to happen. It lessens the likelihood of having to correct the demanding and agitated behaviour of a child who hasn't been pre-warned.

It's helpful to listen carefully to the child and find out what is likely to be tricky about the situation you have identified. Listening to any grumbles and showing you understand (even if you don't agree) is important for gaining cooperation down the line.

There is a balance to be struck between listening to suggestions from the child and being clear about what is and isn't negotiable - it's important to keep the basics of the plan that you had in mind.

Try to keep them busy

There might be special and desirable activities you can suggest to take their mind off the fact that you're unable to provide generous amounts of attention for a while. Where possible include an element of choice of activity for them.

Snatching time for a phone call, for example...

Provide reassurance as you discuss the plan

An example around bedtime...

Drip, drip attention and aim for positivity

As you attend to your task, it may be possible to break off and provide moments of positive verbal attention for following expectations. Making eye contact to show you are still 'connected' or thumbs up and smiles can work well too; these 'non-verbal' ways to encourage good behaviour are helpful in many situations and, for the phone call example, avoid the necessity of breaking off your conversation to give verbal praise.

Offer sweeteners and reward cooperation

Again, it's important to reward what you want to see more of: as we've seen, most of the reward is your attention, but as part of your plan consider other types of rewarding activity after the situation is over and they have done well.

WHEN I'VE FINISHED ON THE PHONE WE'LL GET YOUR SCOOTER OR BIKE OUT AND GO TO THE PARK. WHICH ONE WOULD YOU LIKE TO TAKE?

Talk about the actions you will take if they don't follow your expectations

Sometimes, when unwanted behaviour is hard to crack, it is necessary to include in the preparation a warning of what will happen if they don't cooperate. At other times this more negative element is best left, especially if you sense the positive strategies we mentioned above will work for your child. If in doubt aim to be as positive as possible!

Dealing with difficulties

Remember the plan (but small adjustments can be okay!)

Sticking to the plan you have communicated helps children feel secure in your leadership and the result is more relaxed and cooperative children. Beware rigidity though! On some occasions it can be helpful to modify things a little as you go along so that children can feel they are meeting expectations, even though they haven't done exactly as you requested - especially if it becomes clear that your brief was too difficult!

Respond promptly

When the behaviour slips a little, quick action is needed. If you can, shorten the phone call or whatever you are doing, restate your expectations and refocus your child. Engineer things so that they gain success with their behaviour and achieve their reward:

When your attention has been promised after a given period it is advisable to stick to it, otherwise the attention-driven behaviour will probably flare up again. Setting a timer for all to see can help.

Supporting the child to cooperate and meet expectations (even if you have had to adapt and change the goalposts a little during a tricky moment) and making sure that they get to the set goal in the end will keep things positive and promote better behaviour.

Decisive, low-key action

Making a big deal out of attention-seeking can back-fire; we tend to get more of what we focus on. Parents who take action in a quiet and nonchalant manner when kids are in full flow usually get the results they are looking for.

Avoid allowing attention-seeking behaviour to bubble on or escalate. Some parents feel they should ignore this type of behaviour so their children don't gain the attention they are looking for. Whilst this can work in certain low-level situations, children often find a way of escalating things when they are ignored. Taking prompt action to calmly and assertively prevent it from continuing usually has more impact and, importantly, shows that you are clear with your boundaries. Children who are kindly and confidently prompted to follow their parents' expectations feel more secure and calmer.

Show understanding

Part of the action that you take can be showing your child that you 'get it' and letting them know (with language they understand) that you can see their point. This often 'takes the wind out of their sails' and calms things down, but it should only be brief, as we don't want to reinforce the behaviour that is causing a problem.

Distract

Once you've responded and taken action, it's important to avoid lapsing into a general 'good telling off'. Change the subject and look for ways they can be otherwise occupied.

So...sticking to a basic plan and guiding the child through the situation with a calm, sympathetic and adaptable mindset will help to improve attention-fuelled behaviour. Many other instances of bothersome behaviour will fall into place if the attention seeking issues can be addressed successfully. This can take a big investment of time and effort for a while, and some other jobs might be relegated for the time being. But it is well worth it when things calm down!

Chapter 2: Testing Transitions...

Parents regularly mention behaviour problems when children are prompted to change from one activity or task to another, like going to bed or getting out of the house in time for school. It is common for children to be inflexible when faced with transitions and lots of kids object to being 'moved on' through their day.

It may look like this:

or even:

Children can struggle with single transitions from one activity to another or with getting through a number of transitions in a routine. The more uncertainty there is in a new situation, such as a visit somewhere unknown or facing something different at school, the more the uncooperative behaviour can set in. This can stem from some anxiety about what's about to happen, or a reluctance to get out of a comfort zone. It can purely be unwillingness to stop the enjoyment of a pleasant activity and move on to something less agreeable. Sometimes it is about facing boring, and maybe difficult routines with no nice attention. It could be part of a more general habit of saying no and arguing. Or it might be a combination of any of these things.

Prevention

IN THIS PREPARATION I AIM FOR A MIX OF RELAXED, CONFIDENT 'MATTER OF FACT' EXPLAINING AND SUPPORTIVELY GIVING THEM A BIT OF CHOICE AND CONTROL.

Prepping when 'the going is good'

Preparing the brain when it's in calm, rational mode is a great way of avoiding the most 'heightened' and exhausting behaviour that accompanies attempts to gain cooperation in the stressful transition moments. 'Prepping' doesn't always completely solve the issues later on but can lower emotional states so that at least things become more manageable. It helps to talk through the big or small changes they need to make, including tricky routines and new 'uncomfortable' situations to be faced. This is about getting them ready whilst responsive: before they actually need to make any change(s) and prior to becoming involved in 'doing their own thing'.

Put them in the picture but be mindful of their viewpoint

Summarise what is going to happen, paying particular attention to what it's going to look like from their angle and what is expected of them. What boundaries will you impose and what natural break point can you use in a favoured activity to make it easier for them to see the end point?

Make some offers

Supportively discuss what help they need to make the change(s). What will make it easier? Take on a collaborative 'we're all in it together' approach. Identify the particularly tricky bits and offer support with any of these moments by providing some 'fun' or pleasant solutions or merely providing some of your attention at these points.

Listen and understand

It can be helpful, especially with older, 'more verbal' children, to talk about the issues in a bit more detail and to really listen and address what the child perceives as 'stumbling blocks'. Try a non-judgmental approach, at least to start with, and avoid becoming defensive or explaining your point of view at too early a stage of the discussion.

Only 'lay down the law' after you have listened and showed you have understood their view of things.

Reassurance, choices and fun

Present the prospect of unwanted situations in a confident and encouraging manner. Stress aspects of the situation which are more positive from their perspective and might help them remain calm. Choices within boundaries always support better behaviour so, if it's appropriate, present some pleasant jobs, responsibilities or tasks from which they can select. Keep them busy, let them help and give them something to look forward to at the end.

Pick out the main points

Avoid overburdening young children or those who struggle to remember instructions with too much information ahead of complicated routines/situations.

Support them with managing their own time

Most parents find that giving children a say and some autonomy about how they plan their time and which activities to choose, within clear boundaries, can support better, more cooperative behaviour.

Visuals

Some children respond well to visual 'timetables' which have the elements of the routine listed in image or written form.

The timetable is used as a reminder before the event with attention drawn to it in a 'light-touch', relaxed way, and is used to keep everyone focused through the routine.

Reward systems

Completing and checking off all the tasks can lead to a small, inexpensive reward. This might be a sticker towards a bigger goal such as a treat or a trip, or whatever will motivate the child. A young child needs to experience a desired reward quickly or any system like this will lose its effect. With any reward system to improve behaviour it is worth bearing in mind that, to make a difference, all children need to experience frequent success. The system should have a natural ending after say 3 of the bigger 'goal' rewards being achieved.

Being adaptable

I HAVE FOUND THAT THINKING THROUGH WHAT I NEED HIM TO DO AND ADAPTING MY OWN 'AGENDA' HELPS A LOT. SO IF IT'S POSSIBLE, WHEN I NEED HIM TO STOP DOING SOMETHING I TAKE CARE WITH THE TIMING OF MY INSTRUCTION. I WAIT FOR A GOOD MOMENT.

I ALSO GIVE HIM MORE TIME TO DO WHAT HE NEEDS OR WANTS TO DO, SO I DON'T RUSH HIM. I AVOID A CONFRONTATION IF IT ISN'T NECESSARY.

Despite the benefits of predictably sticking to a shared plan and having clear expectations, an element of flexibility when guiding the child through transitions can be helpful. The aim is to allow room for manoeuvre without seeming to 'back down'.

To this end, take note of where they are in their play/activity and engineer things a little to fit in with them. For example, if it is practicable, wait until they have reached a natural break in their game to make their transition.

Similarly, modifying routines can be a good approach. As an example, allowing plenty of time for the morning routine and avoiding hurrying children through a number of activities is a straightforward step to support better behaviour. Many parents have found that just getting them up ten minutes earlier can promote a calmer atmosphere and enable pleasant activities to be built in to the routine, especially after finishing off the 'boring' tasks.

Countdown

As parents get closer to the transition moment they can encounter resistance, even when the preparation has been exemplary and sensible adaptations have been made. Some kids feel aggrieved at the thought of change no matter what! It is useful to remember that even though there are children who remain stubbornly reluctant during transitions, prior knowledge and being pre-warned in a calm manner will lower emotional levels.

At this point, using clear signals and timescales in the run-up to a transition can reduce irritability, and reinforce the message that you meant what you said when you told them something was going to happen.

EVEN THOUGH I'VE PREPARED MY CHILD BEFOREHAND, I ALSO PROVIDE WARNINGS AND COUNTDOWNS AS THE TRANSITION APPROACHES ...

TEATIME IS IN 5 MINUTES!

TEATIME IS IN 2 MINUTES!

'I'm Just Going to...'

This is used at the last moment and helps children who respond badly to adults standing over them waiting expectantly for, or demanding cooperation, like this...

Inventing a little task for yourself and letting them know that straight afterwards it will be time for action, otherwise known as the 'I'm Just Going to...' strategy, helps the child to process the fact that they do have to stop, and you really mean it, but also that you're not going to be confrontational. It's a breathing space before that dreadful 'doing as you've been asked' thing!

'When...then...'

The 'When...then...' strategy is a good, versatile technique to get children to follow instructions.

The bitter pill of needing to move on to or get through an unappealing activity is sweetened by making some aspect of it enjoyable, or presenting an appealing benefit of completing the transition. This 'carrot' will probably have been dangled as part of your preparation but can also be used 'on the spot' as you are on the point of getting into the situation.

As the parent guides the child through the required change(s), they hold in mind what the child wants, and usually there will be something, whether it's attention or a more 'concrete' reward.

The adult makes the rewarding outcome contingent on the undesirable activity or tricky transition being completed.

In addition, during implementation, being able to make some kind of choice can be motivating and meet the child's need to be independent and have some control.

It is easy to choose the wrong 'carrot' to dangle, and you find it fails to motivate the youngster to make the required transition. A willingness to adopt a new carrot during a situation, one which is 'a need' that they have expressed will help here. As it becomes clear what the child wants, seize on this and promise to deliver when there is cooperation.

As many children, especially younger ones, are motivated by gaining a parent's attention walking away from an uncooperative child can prompt a demand or need to come and find you. At this point a 'when...then...' statement can be effective, especially one that involves some rewarding attention when the child starts to do as asked.

Dealing with difficulties

Compassionate Assertiveness

I NOW KNOW HOW TO ADDRESS UNWANTED BEHAVIOUR PROMPTLY AND FOLLOW THROUGH WITHOUT TOO MUCH DELAY. SO I SHOW THAT I MEAN WHAT I SAY BY TAKING ACTION. I DO THIS CALMLY AND A BIT SYMPATHETICALLY.

I SEEM TO GET RESULTS IF I MAKE THEM DO WHAT I WANT WHILST UNDERSTANDING THAT THEY DON'T WANT TO! AS I DETERMINEDLY POWER THROUGH, I STAY POSITIVE AND DISTRACT THEM. IT DOES TAKE WILLPOWER!

If the right progress is not being made, avoid allowing the child to do their own thing and go against your expectations for too long. Take calm and 'measured' action rather than showing any wobbly tendencies. Hesitancy with following through with what you've said is going to happen can lead to the youngster readily taking the reins, and this taste of control can be habit-forming.

IF I HANG ON LONG ENOUGH, SHE'LL GIVE UP. IT'S ALWAYS THE SAME STORY!

This determined approach is best tempered with some genuine sympathy and understanding for their plight. Moaning can be accepted and appreciated for a short while. This non-confrontational position, which involves a mix of concern with guiding leadership rather than a cajoling, argumentative style, can reduce irritability and de-escalate situations.

On some occasions you may need to voice their annoyance for them. Children can just 'play up' rather than verbalising irritation. Take a guess and say what you think is troubling them whilst showing a bit of genuine understanding.

This 'sympathy' stage shouldn't be overplayed for too long. Tailing it off and replacing it with a quiet, relaxed and determined approach will avoid the danger of the child 'milking' the attention whilst remaining uncooperative.

Move them on afterwards as calmly and confidently as possible. Aim for a 'measured', relaxed manner which gently but firmly stops them doing what they're doing.

If necessary take a moment to prepare yourself before moving in for this assertive engagement and, if you need to, fake the required self-assuredness!

Distract and motivate

Use distraction, add in choices and encouragement, and avoid arguments

Stay as relaxed as you can but hold the line. Use humour if you feel this will work.

The moment your child starts to do as asked, even in a cursory way, use praise to acknowledge their cooperation and take the opportunity to provide something they will find rewarding.

Calm-Down Time

Children who remain uncooperative or unmanageable despite parents' best efforts can benefit from some 'calm-down time'. This is similar to the 'naughty step' approach in that you are removing the child from the difficult situation, but it's different because it is part of a wider picture of engagement and support towards the child being in a calmer state, and it's not designed to be punitive.

When it looks like your child is repeatedly refusing to cooperate or out of control, assertively but gently take them to a nearby quiet spot away from other people and distractions, and begin the calming down process. The first part is staying calm yourself and then you can gently soothe the child if you need to. Let it be known that they can get back into circulation when they begin to calm down or start to follow instructions. Be a little 'neutral' and 'matter of fact' so the child doesn't receive huge amounts of attention; save the dazzling attention for when they turn things around.

The calm-down time steps in more detail

1   Choose a quiet place and gently but firmly take your child there.

2   **Stay and keep things calm**. Firmly but kindly prevent 'out of control' behaviour. Remain fairly quiet, low-key and soothing. Gently hold and stroke your child if this helps.

3   **Make it in their interest to calm down.** Use the promise of something nice when they get themselves together or let it be known they can return to 'normality' as soon as they can do as asked.

4   Praise the smallest signs of calming down and allow them back into circulation.

5   Remain with them and calmly insist they do as they were asked in the first place...firmly direct them to do so.

6   Repeat calm-down time if necessary.... *or*

    Lots of acknowledgement, praise and attention when they make the first steps toward getting it right or cooperating, in any shape or form. Remember more attention for being appropriate than for 'losing it'.

Chapter 3: Emotions Running High...

It can be very wearing (and worrying) when children have frequent outbursts of upset and distress:

It may look like this:

It's a learning curve

It usually helps if parents can see these high emotions as a lack of skills and a need to develop emotional regulation, rather than naughtiness. It takes a long time for all of us to learn to manage frustration, to be considerate of others and deploy calming down strategies. Remind yourself that these 'OTT' emotional responses are very normal for young children and most children learn to tolerate difficult situations as they mature. Some are slightly slower than others to get there. Emotional regulation skills are the subject of lifelong learning!

Prevention

Keep calm and supportive:

Pick up on negative emotion and irritability early

Stay vigilant, and try and identify these signs early so that you can step in and sympathise before it all tips into bad behaviour. A child who struggles to manage their emotions over a goal they didn't score or missing out on a special part in the school play can be supported by adults putting their own thoughts aside and tuning into them promptly. Listening to their upset and accepting that the situation is distressing for them before piling in with our take on things can often be challenging, but works well as a way of lowering emotional levels.

Provide encouragement and support

Even if you are struggling to get your head around how a situation could be so upsetting, it helps if you can support them to appropriately express frustrations and show some understanding and acceptance.

Soothe your child, then encourage and help them to move on. Teach them how to distract themselves and together think of ways to handle a similar issue in the future.

Be aware that difficult, uncooperative behaviour could be about irritability, anxiety or stress

It isn't always easy to recognise upsetting emotions in children and things can often play out in unexpected ways; this emotional 'baggage' may have been carried around for a while, especially if they are likely to react badly over seemingly minor issues. The trigger may not be as obvious as a missed goal!

Picking up early on this stress can be challenging but is worth the effort. Close monitoring and timely interventions can help. The early signs can look like tension in the face; hunched shoulders; clenched fists; whinging; distractibility; being uncommunicative and argumentative. Address this low level discomfort in a gentle way before it escalates by fully engaging with the child and gently and supportively acknowledging their discomfort.

With younger children, or those who find words difficult to come by, it can be helpful to sensitively hazard a guess at the cause of the problem as they may not realise what is upsetting them. Voicing some suggestions about the reasons for their irritability can go a long way in supporting the calming process.

Prepare and support before tricky times

Prior to a situation which has given rise to upset on previous occasions talk supportively with your child so they can think their way into an uncomfortable situation while they are still calm. Talk to them about what to expect and how things may pan out. Include in this chat some easily remembered, simple coping strategies. Stay upbeat and positive but inject some realism and prepare for a worst case scenario.

Together come up with 'a script' to use if they lose a game or if things don't go their way, and prepare and rehearse an appropriate action or two.

Acknowledge Improvements

Notice and praise progress, even a small step in the right direction. If they manage to cope a little more effectively with a tricky situation and there is a better outcome, point out what they did well and commend them for it so that it is more likely to happen next time round.

Boundaries

Children who have outbursts or get upset easily need the security and certainty of clear expectations and structure in their lives.

With a known tricky situation in the offing, it is important to provide structure and clarity just prior to the event, before the child has thought their way into making a demand or gets on a roll of wanting something unrealistic.

Instead of waiting for the bothersome behaviour to begin try to pre-empt things by setting the boundary before a demand is made and before the emotions begin to 'run high'.

Instead of...

Try...

Instead of...

Try...

As you do this preparation and put boundaries in place there may be a need to coach some coping strategies and think through some distraction activities.

If there is whinging as you set the boundary remember the 'sympathy and understanding' response. Gently and genuinely acknowledge that they are disappointed and you can understand why. Don't be tempted to give in though.

Coach and Ref

If your child is prone to losing control during playtime with siblings or friends, be present and prevent the issues by coaching them through interactions and being a leadership presence for a while until your child settles into the play. Start this supervision well before they 'lose it', and take the opportunity to teach them sharing and taking-turns skills.

Consider Pre-emptive Calm-down Time

If you see an emotional outburst about to happen, try stepping in and, calmly and gently, taking your child away from the action before things get out of hand. This isn't about punishment; it is a time to bring their emotional levels down while away from everyone else. The parent can stay with the child and soothe, distract or coach.

Of course all this is only possible if parents stick close by and carefully watch the interaction.

Talk with your child when things are settled about managing their emotions

This is a positive exercise, maybe a recognition that they have coped well and better than expected during a situation.

Or it can be a time to offer a supportive ear and put heads together to look at strategies to help the child stay calm, react positively or be more assertive.

In a more 'ad hoc' way, as opportunities arise, teach them all about emotions. Take opportunities to extend their emotional vocabulary. Discuss your own emotions and those of your family, friends and people on TV and in books. Point out that someone is feeling sad, for example, and discuss why that is and how they cope.

Dealing with difficulties

Help the child to calm down

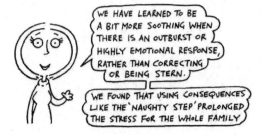

Outbursts can involve hitting out; if this has happened make sure the person who has been harmed in any way is ok. Pay attention, show caring and take action, if necessary, to ensure the person on the receiving end is cared for, emotionally and physically.

At the same time keep your distressed 'super-charged' child safe. If you are able, use calm-down time away from the action. This is a quietly soothing time, rather like when they have had a bit of a tumble, and can include a stroke of the back and not too much fuss. It may seem difficult for some parents to think of soothing a child who has hit out, however aggression is usually about heightened emotions and distress and if we ignore it, begin a 'telling off' or try to reason or teach at this point it will all go over their heads – and it can make things even worse in a highly charged child.

For other disruptive but non-aggressive outbursts a calm-down time in a nearby quiet area can also work well when other tactics haven't worked and further action is required. In fact it is preferable to take this kind of action promptly rather than allowing the child to disturb the home with a meltdown or bubbling resentment. The change of scene, the clear message that you are serious enough to carry out a 'removal' from the action (that you mean business), and the sheer boredom of being with a quiet and neutral parent can bring about a transformation. Remain relaxed yourself in calm-down time, and soothe if necessary, but be just a bit boring in your gentleness (not too much fun). Avoid long discussions at this point; the aim is to calm things down enough to allow a reintroduction into circulation so that appropriate behaviour can be noticed and praised.

Reintroduce the child and support better behaviour

When the child is a little more relaxed and less emotional, acknowledge the effort they have made to calm down. Show you're pleased that things are getting back on track, and let it be known that there can be a return to normal as long as they can manage better, and that you will help with this.

Talk briefly about how to cope with friends or family. Together come up with some solutions. It might be necessary to only expect a short burst of appropriate interaction. If an apology is necessary try to prompt your child to suggest it. Don't push too hard for an apology at this point.

Assertively, but in a relaxed and pleasant way, escort the child back to the same situation or, if that isn't possible, expect calm interaction with others elsewhere.

Stay with them, and focus fully on helping and prompting appropriate social and emotional skills back in the group situation. Be relaxed but firm, and 'make it happen'.

Look for signs of 'normal' interaction, the opposite of the problem behaviour earlier, and praise immediately for getting it even just a little bit right. Don't expect too much! Once there is a sign of success, move on to something more comfortable, especially if things still seem slightly dodgy.

Have a 'debrief' session when things have calmed down

This should be a relaxed and empathic chat, which opens with a gentle question: what happened? Then: tell me more about it. Any answers are listened to and understood without interruption. Asking how their behaviour affected another key player (or victim) can be a good move if the youngster has the requisite skills; an empathic response can be encouraged with a couple of gentle suggestions. It may be necessary to agree an apology if one wasn't made immediately after the incident; or it might be that another way can be found to make up for any harm or damage. Restating expectations, a couple of practical solutions for a similar future situation and a hug can bring this chat to a close.

Chapter 4: Supermarket Sweep!

Here we look at those difficult shopping trips when parents, just aiming to get the job done, have to contend with their children becoming impatient, whingy, demanding and sometimes out of control. In addition there may be the added delight of sensing the disapproval of a few shoppers who seem to be casting aspersions on our parenting skills!

It may look like this:

Prevention

Modify the approach to shopping

WHEN I FIRST ADDRESSED THE SUPERMARKET STRESS, I KEPT SHOPPING TRIPS SHORT AS THINGS HAD BEEN TRULY AWFUL.

YOU COULD SAY THEY HAD 'PREVIOUS' IN ASDA - AND IN MANY SHOPS IN OUR AREA. I WAS A BIT EMBARRASSED, BUT I KNEW I HAD TO TAKE THEM SO I COULD GET ON TOP OF THINGS

Adapting your children's experience and making things more tolerable for them so they don't get bored and irritable is a general behaviour management technique for many situations, including this one. Until things settle down and the behaviour eases, keep shopping trips brief; this will make it more bearable and manageable for you too. Don't give it chance to go downhill.

Prepare for the trip

Children are less likely to misbehave if there is an explanation when they are in a reasonable mood and before the event. When they know the score in terms of structure and expectations, things tend to be calmer.

Allocate some responsibilities

Children often like to help and gain approval by joining in and taking some responsibility. This tactic also helps to occupy the mind so there's no room for thinking about mischief.

Learn to say 'no' from the start (in a nice way!)

Children frequently wind their parents up in the shops as they pester for things, and it has been known for parents to give in! Children learn quickly that if they 'go on' for long enough parents will surrender in the hope of an easy life. In this situation, the parents have helped to cause the problem. The solution: be clear and definite from the very start and mean it. Tell them what they can and can't have before they become 'attached' to an idea, so well before entering the shop.

Think your way into being definite...

Split your focus - the shopping <u>and</u> the children

Children behave badly in shops sometimes because their parents' attention is elsewhere. Making sure they are getting enough 'good attention' makes it more likely there'll be good behaviour.

This means really 'being with' the child rather than thinking wholly about the shopping. Some of the 'shopping thinking' is best done beforehand so that attention can be focused on the interaction.

Praise

As in other situations, looking for the behaviour you want and acknowledging it 'reinforces' and maintains it.

Dealing with Difficulties

Address issues at an early stage and refocus attention

Act promptly so that the unwanted behaviour doesn't linger on or escalate and become increasingly negative.

As soon as there is a hint of demanding, irritating or 'out of control' behaviour calmly and quietly restate your expectations, and distract.

Adding the caring touch can work wonders; this is a moment where you listen to their point of view or express sympathy for their plight. Follow this up with another dose of distraction.

Take decisive action

If further action is needed this is best done as soon as it's clear the refocusing and distraction hasn't worked. This involves a firmer warning and then 'following through' (taking action) with something the child isn't keen on. This 'consequence' of the behaviour works best when it isn't 'over the top' and can take place immediately.

If things escalate after the warning take immediate decisive, purposeful action.

As you firmly 'make it happen' it may be necessary to get through your shopping quickly and make your escape.

Try to remain calm and power through without being angry or just giving up.

Ploughing on through the shopping in a determined, 'matter-of-fact' way may prompt the child to calm a little, and as it becomes clear that all isn't lost, try distraction (a pleasant change of subject) and go for re-engagement. However, if this attempt at getting things back on track doesn't work, it's important to avoid paying lots of attention to continuing difficult behaviour.

Debrief and repeat

AS WITH ANY OTHER BEHAVIOURAL INCIDENT, THE LAST PART OF 'DEALING WITH IT' IS THE DEBRIEF SESSION.

AFTER A DIFFICULT SHOPPING TRIP, I LEAVE A GAP AND CHOOSE A MOMENT AFTER ON THE SAME DAY WHEN EVERYONE IS CALMER. WE ADDRESS THE PROBLEM AND I TRY TO SUPPORT MY CHILD TO MANAGE BETTER NEXT TIME. I TELL HIM WE ARE GOING BACK TOMORROW, OR VERY SOON, AND THIS IS WHAT I EXPECT...

OKAY, WHAT HAPPENED IN THE SUPERMARKET EARLIER?

WELL, I WANTED SWEETS!

OKAY, I CAN SEE THAT THE SWEETS LOOKED GOOD. LET'S THINK HOW WE CAN MAKE THINGS BETTER WHEN WE GO BACK THIS AFTERNOON - THERE WON'T BE ANY SWEETS.

SO WHAT CAN WE DO SO YOU CAN FORGET ABOUT THE SWEETS?

So have a review of what happened last time, and talk about what could be done differently to avoid problems in the future. Bite the bullet and try again with a quick shopping trip shortly after difficulties have occurred. Remember, short and sharp will support your child to behave better as there will be less opportunity for them to lose the plot. Repeat expectations before you enter the shop. Give them jobs, pay attention and insist they do as asked.

Then celebrate success!

Chapter 5: Food, glorious food!

Young children, and some older kids, can have genuine difficulty with trying new foods and like to stick to the old favourites. This can cause conflict and frustration in the family. In addition, mealtimes can be used as attention and control-seeking opportunities. Parents may become anxious about their child's eating habits and kids learn to call the shots when it becomes clear to them that it means so much to mum and dad to get that spoonful of peas, or whatever, down the hatch, and in this situation almost any behaviour is tolerated. For some families mealtime behaviour is just an extension of the poor behaviour at other times.

It may look like this:

Prevention

Structure - regular snacks and meals

Establishing some boundaries around 'grazing' or going to the cupboard whenever children feel at a loose end can be helpful in getting on top of mealtime issues. Rules to prevent grazing are often effective as the issues may result from being constantly topped up with food and therefore not hungry and not motivated to get through meals. As usual, tell them of any new rules when things are calm and prior to any hunger pangs.

Having the structure of regular and frequent snacks and meals takes the stress out of establishing some 'order' at mealtimes. It means that children will get fed often and won't go hungry if they are asked to leave the table because of their behaviour. It also gives a clear message that the parents are in charge!

Involvement and Choice

Giving children a role in meal planning, shopping and preparation, and creating fun and enjoyment around all of this can help kids feel more 'attached' to the food that is put in front of them and less likely to be 'dismissive' and difficult when it comes to eating.

If it's convenient, allow some choice from a limited menu. This can be helpful to reduce 'pickiness' or controlling behaviour during the meal.

I GIVE HIM CHOICES BEFORE I PREPARE ANYTHING

TUNA OR CHEESE SANDWICHES FOR LUNCH?

NEITHER! I WANT CHOCOLATE SPREAD!

YES, THAT WOULD BE NICE, BUT WE AREN'T HAVING THAT TODAY.

I UNDERSTAND I'VE ALLOWED YOU THAT BEFORE AND IT'S HARD WHEN THINGS CHANGE, BUT THOSE ARE THE CHOICES

≈SIGH≈ OKAY, DAD...

Make it clear before the meal what you expect, and that you are going to take action for misbehaviour, and precisely how that might play out.

For children who tend to refuse to eat what is given to them let them know in advance there is only one meal. If they don't want to eat it they will be able to leave the table but there is nothing else. Sounds harsh, but it can be delivered (and implemented) in a gentle way.

It is sometimes necessary to break up instructions or expectations into chunks so a young child, or one who has difficulty with processing information, can take it all in.

Presenting expectations in pictures (as well as words) can be helpful for children who don't process verbal information too well.

It may be useful to repeat elements of your expectations just before the unwanted behaviour starts. This can be a tricky judgment and definitely needs a watchful eye so the reminder is well-timed and prevents the behaviour. Sensing when the child is heading towards difficulty and gently and quietly reminding, then quickly changing tack and moving into distraction (changing the subject to something interesting) is a good way to head off problems. It is best to avoid continually repeating expectations after the unwanted behaviour has already started as this provides 'reinforcing' attention for negative behaviour, which makes matters worse.

Provide good attention, and choice

Sit with them

Even if you don't eat yourself be present with your kids at mealtimes to provide positive attention and maintain boundaries. Talking about something other than the food and focusing on other subjects can help to prevent children from lapsing into some difficult behaviour. Emphasis on what is and isn't being eaten may result in children sensing the chance to control things and gain a lot of attention because their parents care so much about their food consumption.

Serving themselves

Sometimes conflict occurs because the parent serves up too much food and a big negotiation ensues about how many more forkfuls to eat, giving the child a lot of attention for a negative stance. If children serve themselves this is less likely to happen, especially if there is a rule that they need to eat what is on their plate.

As they serve themselves don't be tempted to comment and cajole about their choices.

Focus on the positive

Look hard for signs that your child is not doing the annoying things that have previously been a feature of mealtimes. Grasp at straws if necessary and give attention for the tiniest improvement in behaviour. Without delay, say something about their more appropriate actions.

Use 'super praise' sometimes, even if this means that you 'lay it on thick'. Make sure this celebration of progress sounds genuine.

In this way descriptive, specific approval (not just a vague 'good boy', 'good girl'), mixed with statements which build self-esteem (describing strengths, qualities, skills or effort) will let your child know what behaviour gets attention. They will feel valued and realise they don't have to misbehave to get a reaction or to make themselves feel important.

Dealing with Difficulties

Warn and then take calm action

Be sure to do what you said would be the consequence of the bothersome behaviour, for example if you said they would have to leave the table, make sure this is what happens.

However, calmly and politely give a warning first...

Immediately after the warning, distract by changing the subject

Make the distraction diverting, something which will capture their interest and has a chance of changing the way they are thinking.

Catch them doing the right thing quickly after the warning

Take notice of any small signs of a turnaround in the behaviour and use praise, so that there is 'reinforcing' attention for the things you want to see.

Follow through

If after the warning the behaviour happens once more (even if it's slightly different, or more minor in nature) gently tell the child they have to leave the table. Stay relaxed and matter of fact; there's no need to be stern. Any strong emotion will give attention and reinforce the unwanted behaviour.

As your child leaves the table, redirect them to do something else

There is no need for another sanction or any disapproval because leaving the table was the consequence. So a diverting activity can be offered, or they may need soothing if upset.

You might be required to stand firm about no additional food until the next snack, and this can mean a combination of riding the storm, distracting and a touch of gentle understanding of their point of view. Avoid giving in on the pudding!

Calm-Down Time

If the behaviour escalates and becomes disruptive or persistently defiant use calm-down time, with a bit of 'when...then...' (see Chapter 2 for an explanation of these approaches).

If the behaviour starts up again repeat calm-down time.

When you are having to take action to stop bothersome behaviour around food and mealtimes stay focused on providing more attention when the behaviour is appropriate (shine a light on it!) and aim for a relaxed and neutral manner as you 'follow through'.

Chapter 6: Car Share Cacophonies

Car journeys are another situation where bothersome behaviour can occur, and it's not easy to deal with in a confined space!

It may look like this:

Prevention

Early communication about what is going to happen, and expectations

It's useful to give some basic information about how long the journey is likely to take, and based on what has caused problems in the past, you can set out some expectations.

Keep them busy, even on short journeys

Make sure they are occupied with things they enjoy so they don't become bored and whingy. Part of their experience should be enjoying a considerable amount of your positive attention. The car is a good place to have some fun together; play games and have a chat.

Ring the changes so that they are able to do a range of activities on a long journey. Include screen time if that will keep you all sane, but have some boundaries around it (expressed beforehand).

Take breaks on long journeys

Everyone needs these, and they can be built in to your expectations, or 'when...then..' communications from chapter 2 as part of the preparation for the journey.

Consider a coin system on a long journey

Set this up with them beforehand. Let them know they will each be awarded 5p or 10p pieces (or whatever coin denomination will work best for your situation) towards holiday money or a treat during/after the journey when they are 'caught being good' on the journey. This means following your rules and generally being pleasant and calm. Be encouraging and upbeat and let them know that you are sure they will earn money to buy some treats - you can talk to them about what they will buy. However, if they can't do as asked they will lose coins too.

This is predominantly a positive reward system and it is crucial that they begin any journey with lots of positive reinforcement. The coin awards are recorded by you (if you're able) as you go along on a piece of paper or on your phone. Or the children can record them (but keep a tally in your head). So at regular and frequent intervals, when the behaviour is ok, use praise and generously award coins.

Keep this reward system on the front burner as best you can so it is meaningful and motivating.

Try to keep the tally fairly even and award jointly as much as possible; avoid setting one up against the other; it's not supposed to be a competition!

More about using the system to manage difficult behaviour in a bit.

If these positive and pro-active strategies don't work and behaviour starts to 'bubble':

Address minor issues quickly

Try to think what is underpinning the first stirrings of discontent and step in. Are they bored, tired, hungry, lacking attention, irritable because of the close proximity of someone who is gaining more attention than them ... or something else? Or a combination of things? Get their attention and ask (nicely), or tentatively take a guess at what might be the cause. Show interest; try not to be grumpy. Listen and do something to address the issues before behaviour gets out of hand.

Distract

Think of a new game/conversation/music. Have some standby engaging activities up your sleeve for such occasions.

141

Dealing with Difficulties

Take prompt action

Avoid allowing unwanted behaviour to become established in the car as this can become a safety problem quite quickly.

Calmly and assertively restate expectations if distraction and sympathy hasn't worked. Don't be afraid to stop the car and turn round so they can see your face and hear it clearly. This shows you really mean what you say.

If the behaviour continues, give a warning of a 'proportionate' consequence.

Avoid an over-reaction. Keep things 'measured' and 'rational' by acting promptly in line with the plan you have made and communicated with the child -this will prevent emotions boiling over which worsens bothersome behaviour.

Instead of: Try:

It's very important that the consequence you use is one that you can deliver quickly and easily - taking into account the enclosed space of the car and everyone needing to get to the destination! This is why something like the coin system can also work as a consequence for bad behaviour, by taking coins away

Follow through as soon as the behaviour happens again

....but try not to get into a 'downward spiral' of taking away more and more cash - have a limit of two coins. If you aren't using the coin system, or the behaviour escalates beyond taking 2 coins, have other consequences at hand. You might consider taking a toy away until the behaviour improves or calmly and nonchalantly stopping the car and saying you won't continue until things are calm.

Get back towards positivity as soon as possible

After implementing a consequence look for any small sign of improved behaviour and comment on it - even if this means clutching at straws!

It's helpful to make it worthwhile for them to stop the difficult behaviour...

Use a lot of praise and 'super quality' attention immediately they show signs of being back on track.

Chapter 7: Collective chaos!

A common complaint from adults is that they find the chaos of having more than one misbehaving child in their care too hard to manage.

It may look like this:

Prevention

Be present and provide leadership

Staying around and interacting with children in situations that have previously been problematic is the first step.

Providing good attention, supervising, mediating and letting them know what is expected during these times all sounds a bit bossy but helps to get 'anarchic' children into better habits.

Only leave when things look pretty settled.

Keep 'an eye and ear out'

When things are calm and it's safe to leave them in settled activities don't go too far. Remain 'tuned in' to the kids' interaction and check in regularly.

Comment on appropriate behaviour

Dipping in and out of a calm scene providing genuine appreciation of the better behaviour will motivate your children to keep going and help reinforce and maintain that settled behaviour.

Parents are sometimes reluctant to break the spell when all is peaceful, reasoning that their presence may trigger some unwanted behaviour. Although a downturn in behaviour may occasionally accompany parent attention, the benefits of positive recognition and good feedback outweigh the risks of ignoring appropriate interaction. It's worth taking a chance and 'going for it' because whatever you pay attention to will be strengthened.

Prepare yourself and have a plan for potentially challenging situations

Tell yourself to be a strong and clear presence as you prepare to manage awkward or chaotic situations and when you need to ask your kids to follow instructions. Approach previously difficult situations in a confident, self-assured and organised way.

Check that you intend to issue clear expectations and you have praise statements at the tip of your tongue for the moment things begin to run smoothly. Is there a 'carrot' you can dangle, a promise of something rewarding, to mark calm behaviour and cooperation? Be clear in your mind what measures you will take to address any ongoing 'trouble'.

Carry out your plan

Positive and strong does it! Give clear countdowns and warnings of any imminent transition, making sure each child understands what is required. Take the lead and follow through, orchestrating the situation for as long as it takes to get what you want. As you do so, keep things as upbeat as possible.

Proximity praise

Tackling the minor misdemeanours of one child can be as simple as providing 'positive strokes' and good attention to a nearby child who is being calm and cooperative: this can turn things around as the unsettled child learns the appropriate way to gain attention.

Dealing with Difficulties

Firm, no-nonsense but non-confrontational

When the behaviour becomes difficult attempt to remain the rational, relaxed adult 'on a mission'; avoid taking the behaviour personally.

Be unambiguous and clear about what you want to happen. If possible initially address all of them as a group; be in charge of the room or situation. Try to think in terms of the tasks that need doing rather than jumping to telling children off too quickly. Catch anyone doing the right thing, comment and thank them.

Give short instructions - quietly, then distract

If possible, put a stop to disruptive or disrespectful behaviour in a low-key, determined way, avoiding drawing too much attention to it. Instead of a 'telling off', which can make behaviour worse and take precious time better used for monitoring things in a strong, upbeat way, try a short quiet instruction to halt the behaviour, This can be followed promptly by a refocusing instruction and distracting 'job'. If more than one child is misbehaving calmly 'pick off' one at a time, prioritising the most disruptive behaviour. Use praise immediately a child turns round their behaviour, even in a perfunctory way. Remove any child who is out of control to a slightly quieter area, whilst continuing to supervise the others as best you can. When a child has been 'wronged' be clear that you will deal with it and you are taking it seriously.

Thanking your child

Finishing off an instruction with a 'thanks' is magic! Children are lulled into believing they accept the instruction, even if they haven't quite managed to bring themselves to cooperate just yet! And if they have cooperated it models respectful behaviour and keeps things positive.

If there has been an 'incident'...

Sometimes incidents can happen without being seen, and there is an upset child to deal with. This creates the challenge of dealing with what's happened to that child and at the same time keeping an eye on the whole group. Go to the child, remain calm and collected and show sympathy without necessarily getting on board and too involved in the 'whys and wherefores' at this point; whilst you attend to the child direct the others and give them some positive attention when they do as asked.

If it is clear that the child has been hit, tell them you will talk with them more about it and deal with it when everyone is settled and calm. It's important to get to the bottom of exactly what happened, especially before blaming anybody, but this is best done when things are calmer.

Debrief Sessions

Addressing concerning behaviour later when things have settled down and the children are more responsive is important in preventing a repeat performance. They learn much more from a calm discussion than trying to sort it out when everyone is 'uptight'.

Have quiet one-on-one chats to ask what happened, from their angle. Dig deep and attempt to listen non-judgmentally. This acceptance helps children to be upfront and less defensive. Children learn to manage better when they feel 'heard' and emotionally in a good place. So it's worth keeping our own negative emotions in check and staying calm and engaged through these conversations. This doesn't mean we condone poor behaviour; it is important that they see the error of their ways and are encouraged to seek solutions for next time and make amends in their own way.

It is useful to have a 'laying down the law' aspect of the debrief session. This is about re-stating expectations and comes after the sympathy and support bit. Children are more likely to learn better ways of behaving if they have had their say without being shouted down or interrupted to let them know what a shambles they have made of things.

Even the 'laying down of the law' bit works best when delivered supportively. There are always reasons for children's behaviour and it is worth giving them the message that, whilst you don't like the behaviour, you understand what was happening for them, you care about them and will help them in future. They're only kids!

After a difficult incident stay vigilant and be present the next time. Coach and prompt them in similar subsequent situations.

Chapter 8: Pulling it all together!

You've been through a lot of detail, so this final chapter is a summary of some of the main ways in which to approach things if you want the behaviour of your children to be less bothersome.

Much of it boils down to:

Communication that works

Build the relationship with your child. Have nice times together. Make positive attention and pleasant chat the biggest part of your communication.

Positive Pie

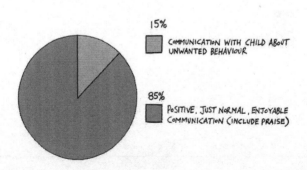

15%
COMMUNICATION WITH CHILD ABOUT UNWANTED BEHAVIOUR

85%
POSITIVE, JUST NORMAL, ENJOYABLE COMMUNICATION (INCLUDE PRAISE)

Try thinking about and reviewing your communication with your child as a 'pie chart'. Aim to stay in the 'bigger slice' and get back there after any correction (which should be over and done with as quickly as possible).

Showing them how to do it

Teach them how to be a 'calm and collected' person by being one yourself.

Giving them a bit of autonomy

Allow your child to be independent and lead their own play and activities when it is appropriate for them to do so. Try and adopt the mindset that playtime is often a good moment to let them be the boss (with this approach they'll be more likely to let you be the boss on other, more pressing occasions).

Preparing

When facing a potentially problematic time prepare your children, when they're calm.

Tell them:

- What's going to happen

- Your expectations and rules

- That you understand their 'gripes'

- That you will make some allowance for their gripes

- They can have some choices within your boundaries

It's often a good idea to repeat some elements of this immediately before the situation (especially the rules - what they can and can't do).

Teaching and supporting

During challenging times when things are likely to go 'pear-shaped' be 'present', interact with them, coach and distract. Praise them for getting it right.

168

Here are some things which generally don't work:

-'telling them off'/lecturing

-reminding, nagging and pleading

-ignoring them when they are being good

-threatening huge consequences or 'distant' sanctions way down the line which you lose the will (or forget) to implement.

- aggressive responses, put downs or sarcasm

- explaining or pleading whilst letting things get out of hand

- saying 'no' and then changing your mind

... and finally, things to remember when the difficult behaviour begins:

Understanding

Show compassion for them when they get it wrong, even if you are really irritated and on edge (this is the trickiest bit!). Do this gently, genuinely and without fuss. Think of possible reasons for the behaviour and quietly put this into words for them. It's about hazarding a guess at the underlying reasons and being sympathetic for a short while. To avoid paying too much attention to unwanted behaviour, move purposefully through this stage and don't get stuck pitying a child who continues to misbehave.

Action!

Take measures to stop bothersome behaviour in its tracks at an early stage. Be calm and take 'proportionate' action which doesn't come as a surprise.

A warning about the consequence of unwanted behaviour is good; but where there is aggression it is important to take immediate action.

Use the 'when...then...' technique to prompt appropriate behaviour. What do they want to do? What do they want you to do? Whatever it is, it won't happen until they do the right thing (the behaviour you want). Not bribery... just establishing your boundaries!

It might be necessary to take something away from them as a consequence. Give it back when they start to show you they can get things right.

Praise with alacrity and pay positive attention immediately they turn their behaviour around!

When there is an improved atmosphere or mood after an unwanted episode expect your child to show that they have learnt how to behave appropriately (and if necessary, make amends). Support them to do this and comment with enthusiasm when they show positive signs or small steps to better interaction and cooperation.

Debrief:

For any repeated unwanted behaviour, when you sense their skills would benefit from more teaching, it can be helpful to tackle things again later still. Ask and help them to answer the following questions:

- What happened?
- What were you thinking/feeling at the time?
- What do you think the other people were thinking?
- What can we do to make sure it won't happen again?
- Do we need to do more to make things better (or make amends)?
- How can I help?

Make sure, where possible, they face a similar situation shortly afterwards so they practise their skills (with your support).

Some children respond better to a debrief which makes use of visual representations rather than just talking.

Good luck from Mandy and Kent. Go for it!

Acknowledgements:

It would not have been possible to write this book without the help of many people – not least, all the children, parents, schools and colleagues Mandy has worked and learned with over the years.

Special thanks to Paul who checked through manuscripts and advised with his customary sensitivity, wisdom and care - Mandy appreciates his support, and not just when she is writing a book!

Thanks to Ellie and Nick for their help and support and for allowing us to practise a few of these strategies (and some less effective ones) when they were little, and for not kicking up too much fuss.

Sorry we didn't always know what we were doing back then. Love you always!

The endorsements from Heather, Madeleine and James are very much appreciated. Thanks for taking the time to read and consider the book, and for being so complimentary.

Kent, you've brought the ideas to life and injected lots of fun! I've appreciated your creativity and reassurance, grateful thanks from Mandy.

We are grateful to Terry for all his patient and conscientious work getting this book into shape.

Lee, a big thank you for a great front cover.

Big thanks to Mandy for her support and patience, from Kent.